A SOJOURNER'S JOURNEY TO TRUE GOD

A SELF TESTIMONY TO GLORIFY GOD

DANIYYEL CHALAK
AMBADAS CHALAK

I dedicate this book to my beloved dearest mother, my family and my well-wisher Chakri sir.

Contents

Foreword

I am one of the reader of the books published by the author, I found the simplicity and naturalistic style of writing in the simple vocabulary and grammar, makes the reader to understand the content intention which the author tries to express.

Preface

I feel pleasure to introduce myself to you as a born again believer in christ since 2012 which is my year of born again in spirit. I feel happy to share my experience with my God, through the words from my heart which make me to be thankful always to my lord for the wonderful transformation occured in my life made me to share my Testimony with you and the world around.

In this book , I Testify the way the God has chosen me to open my blindfolded eyes of mind, the circumstances appointed iby him in my life when i was in a helpless , hopeless state by other earthly Gods. I narrated all the works of God and his miracles does in my family life which lead to the WAY OF SALVATION through Grace of Our Lord Jesus Christ.

Acknowledgements

I thank to my supreme God for the Wisdom and Knowledge granted to me to write this book.

Prologue

The narration belongs to the timeline of 2012 year, where many turns took place in my life under the plan of God implemented in my family through appointing agonic circumstances, by which God made his revelation which lead to the Salvation of God.

This book has the narration of my Personal Testimony written to Glorify the True God with an obesiance and thanks giving.

CHAPTER I

My Days of life before knowing Christ- My PAST

I am Ambadas, the author of this book. I belong to a Indian Hindhu family which is bounded with all the cultures and traditions followed strictly along with the people around. I am a man of Pious since from child hood as I was grown up in the followings of my mother, a great follower of traditions and customs in the religion of Hindhuism.

Since from the childhood till the year of 2012, I too followed and participated all the customs of the traditions like offering the sacrfices to deities in temple, worshipping etc. Before I knew christ, I enjoyed the pleasures like watching movies, moving with the different kinds of people around, involving in their conversations, movements, habits etc as a complete earthly man.

I born in a family in 1994 whera my father is a simple workmen of leather and also a shoe mender and my mother was an house-wife and also assisatant to my father in his work. My complete Education starting from my Secondary grade to Bacherlors pursued in home state Telangana. I had a sister 3years younger to me. This is my a brief intro.

CHAPTER II

Negligence shown at Good news about the Savior

In my Family my mother somewhere in her hearts corner, she had a mustard seed of faith. So yearly once on the occasion of christmas, our familly used to visit the church as a Yearly Christians, but not as Christian. In our streets locality many christians of churches as procession went before me, distributing the tracks (Gospel Pamplets about Jesus) to all the people in the streets, on roads in the Christmas season, Good Friday, Easters day occassion. Many tracks approached to my hand, their voices and messages about Christ also came upto my ear, but I neglected completely as I am completely immersed and blindfolded with the follow of statutes and false faith of the earthly deities.

I never thought of why the people from the churches participate in the procession distributing the message about Lord Jesus christ. The procession includes all status of people, rich, poor, Employees, God Servants etc. Just casually like a news paper I read the Gospel tracks, but I never thought in depth regarding the message which God wish to speak to me.

I never realized the importance and worth of Gods message which approached me, instead I took it in a negligent and careless manner. But in fact God always had a plan to save the perishing souls. It will be implemented untill the time has fulfilled. The time may come in the form of circumstances, tough situations.

CHAPTER III

God's plan initiated in behind through circumstances

But one day in month of July 2012 my dad heavily consumed wine and he came to home at late night. Then after sometime he started quarrelling, scolding, making noise in my home and at last he went out of home in drowsiness with anger. My mother felt fed up with my dad and she left to think of him and continued we our daily life. But my mother waited for my father that he come back again. But 3 days passed away, he didn't return back to home, then I and my mother felt afraid and made calls to my uncles (brothers of my mother) and told everything that happened and she told to make an immediate enquiry of my father existence. They too felt shocked on hearing the news about missing of my father. Then they started to inform all their contacts to inform them as soon as they find any piece of information about my father. My mother went into depression and became nervous without having the food and water. I searched all the regular places where my father used to visit, but I didn't found him. I asked all the people who move close to him, but they replied that they too didn't seen him.

CHAPTER IV

Helpless earthly deities- Blind eyes reopened

Then my mother out of depression she started to pray the earthly Gods and deities she worshipped since from her childhood, to make my father to return back to home, but no response we heard from any corner of the town or people around. Since from many days even though we were in Hindu religion my mother in her corner of her heart had a mustard seed of faith towards Lord Jesus Christ. Now in her last attempt of faith, she started praying to Jesus Christ to reveal the place where my father is and also to make him to bring back to home. When she ended her prayer after few hours we received a call from one of the contacts of my uncle, news regarding my father, that he had seen my father in a Govt. Hospital in an unconscious, extreme emergence condition. Then we astonished for a while and we rushed to Hospital along with my uncles.

CHAPTER V

God lead us in the bitter times to reach sweet Salvation

The actual matter we come to know after reaching the hospital, that this incident took place on the day he left from home in a rainy climate. He was walking along the road in the rain, suddenly a car in a reverse direction didn't noticed my father behind the car, gave a jerk to him. Then at that instant he fell back on road, causing an hit by road on backside of head, and felt on road unconscious whole night, due to this his whole body, nerves got freeze and the blood temperature down felled. Along with this half of the body got paralyzed .Suddenly an ambulance came from that way (may be people nearby may be called) in the late night noticed my father. They picked him up and took to nearby Govt. Hospital.

Then we asked the doctor about his condition and recovery, then he replied they can't handle the case as the situation is worse and due to non-availability for necessary aid, equipment's for treatment. They advised to take to other hospital. Then we took him in an ambulance immediately and rushed to Gokul Multi specialty Private Hospital nearby. Then the doctor of the hospital examined and suggested for CT scan for clear cause of the current condition. So we took him for diagnosis and the reports shown that there is a cut in the one of the nerves in the brain causing the blood leakage and in some areas there is existence of blood clots. This may be the cause of his state he is in now. Then the doctor advised us and forwarded the case to Yashoda Hospital as the condition is getting worse time to time. The time at that moment is nearly 9.30 PM.

Then we booked an ambulance and drive to referred Hospital in Hyderabad, we reached the destiny 11.00PM. My mother was praying continually with heart burden till we reached hospital. The doctor on duty at night of that hospital said after reading the report of the previous hospital, they don't have exact equipment's and specialists to treat the case. They forwarded the case to Image Hospital near Ameer pet, Hyderabad.

The doctors of Image Hospital, looked at the report and examined my father condition. They admitted and opened case sheet, whole night we spent there along with my uncles. In the morning the doctors said nearly (One) 1Lakh rupees must be required to perform the surgery immediately. Then we felt shocked as we don't had such amount at that instant. Neither my uncles had. Then we asked doctor for some time to pay, but he said immediately must be paid, as surgery must be underwent immediately. So we were thrown in the dilemmatic state. The time at that moment is nearly 9.00PM. Then one of my uncle advised to shift to Osmania General Hospital at Afzalgunj.

CHAPTER VI

Witnessed God's Helping Hand

We moved to the Osmania Hospital, reached by 9.00PM. The GODS ACTS STARTED FROM NOW...and things went on faster.

Act-1:

As we reached, the doctors available in the emergency room, **_they examined, admitted, opened a case sheet and ordered the sub doctors to prepare the Operation theatre._**

Act-2

The doctor said the patient need a B+ve Blood immediately to carry out surgery. Then I and my uncles dispersed out went in search and tried for blood, but they returned empty hand. Then one of my uncles friend work there as ward boy. He met my uncle and asked what happened? Why he was here? Then uncle replied the need of B+ve Blood. Then he said, don't worry I will get it for you with my influence. He took no money for it. **_The blood is arranged by Lords Grace_**. As per the fact it is very tough to get the blood at that time.

My mother continued her prayer from beginning of taking my father into operation theatre. Before the doctors made ready for the operation they spoked to us that they cannot give any assurance of his survival and life. They asked us to sign on the paper as per the formal procedure everywhere happens. My mother signed on paper with a water filled eyes, out bursting pain. The Doctors took my father in an unconscious state. The surgery went on and finished by 11.00PM, they took him out of the theatre and placed him on the bed in Neural Patients ward. We were so tensed about my father.

<u>Act-3</u>

As soon as he was laid on the bed, ***immediately he was back to conscious state by the grace of God*** which is for sure a MIRACLE and WORK of GOD. We were shocked and amazed, because the co-patient care takers near to bed told to us that, it is very less chances for survival of a patient after a Neural Surgery as it is very delicate and with less hope. But unto God everything is possible. The Lord heard my mother's cry, prayer and did Miracle before our sight.

<u>My Mother Vow Unto GOD,</u>

When my father was taken into an operation theatre my mother made a prayerful vow to God that "I will believe and follow you (Jesus), if you save him from death bed by making operation success".

<u>My Career Paused For Father</u>

My career was paused, because during the time of this incident, EAMCET counselling was going on, as I finished my Intermediate Education and appeared for EAMCET exam. At those days this incident took place and took me into a great turn. I least bothered my career which I considered as worthless before my father situation.

<u>The Horrible Days I Spent...</u>

I and my mother spent 15 days in the Osmania Hospital taking care of my father. My mother look after my father inside ward, I stay out of ward to go to and fro to different sections of Hospital to assist my mother like submitting the samples of my father for test, bringing the reports, food and other purposes. The days which I spent in that Hospital is very horrible can't be expressed in a line of sentence. I used to consume my lunch, dinner in the corridor, near to the ward. During that time sometimes the dead bodies were carried from behind me when I was eating. I forgot to bath daily as I was not in stable state to look after myself. My only focus and aim at that moment revolves in my mind is to take back my father in a recovered state to home by making him to walk.

I used to sleep inside the ward under the bed of father. My mother always laid an eye on my father because, we tied his hand and legs to bed to prevent him from disturb the surgery stitches on his head. He sometimes moved into mental disorder behaving abnormal. Sometime my mother had a sleepless night by looking after my father. The days which we spent on hospital never had a thought of what we ate, how we are. One of my uncle stays in Hyderabad used to bring the food for us two times a day.

The days passed on, daily I and my mother made an exercise to my father in walking step by step to bring movement in the paralyzed legs. We both used to take him to attend the wash room. Like a baby we served and took care of my father.

The days passed on, we did all the things in regular schedule without fail since from morning rise of sun to sunset till we see moon at night. God helped our struggling hands and touched my father, slowly some improvement we noticed I my father. His paralyzed limbs responding slowly, also he is recognizing us, speaking, eating something easily, which is not so earlier.

I used to struggle a lot to make him to eat food, I used to sit behind him while eating when he didn't had strength in his backbone. He used to hold spoon in mouth, spit away the chew food, sometime slapped mother and me when we tried to feed him. We bear everything as we aimed his recovery.

<u>The day of relieve...</u>

At last as we are approaching the 15th day, found some improvements than day one. But still he is under paralyzed state. This made the doctors to discharge my father. So we felt happy and took one year medicines and started back to the home town.

CHAPTER VII

God Reminded about the leftover past

We reached our home, all the neighbor's felt happy and astonished at Gods work. The early Hindu God deity portraits, idols were there in my house which we left unnoticed. Daily we took care of my father as we did in Hospital. But one fine day, all of sudden he was attacked by fit, started behaving abnormal, throwing all the nearby things away, hitting the persons nearby. There was an aunty beside my house, she was a Christian. My mother went to her and requested to her to come and pray for my father. Then she came inside and looked around and said to my mother in a raised voice **"first of all you go and throw away those portraits and idols from your house"**.

Then my mother realized the cause of my father behavior. It was raining at that time. The aunty prayed and applied prayed oil to my father fore head. My mother took all the idols, portraits in a bag on bare feet she walked to nearby temple, placed all of them at a tree. She came back to home, and shocked to see my father sleeping peacefully.

CHAPTER VIII

God's Hand Helped Once Again

After a few days passed, we noticed a swelling in the region where the surgery was done. Again his situation getting worse. We felt panic and decided to visit the Hospital again. So we booked a car, took my father along with my uncles rushed to hospital. The treated Doctor examined and there is a puss formation in the swelled area. So he said he must be admitted again, also once again a small surgery to be done to clear the formed puss. Then my mother prayed strongly to Lord Christ, *"Oh Lord the previous surgery is made by the man, so now you should do operate on my husband, you perform the surgery"*. Then the surgery went on, the puss suction pipe is inserted into section of head where surgery is made. We stayed a month again. The pus cleared from the swelled area, became normal. Thus Lord made the operation success.

The Doctors assured he will be fine and discharged father. We came back to our home. From that day onwards he started recovering slowly, we believed the Lord's hand is upon my father.

CHAPTER IX

Day of Confession-Rebirth

<u>My rock past heart didn't melted....</u>

Coming to my situation, though I have seen all these with my eyes, my rock heart didn't accepted Jesus as my savior. I restarted my career as Graduate, so I joined in a Degree college near in same town.

<u>Day of Confession</u>

The Christian aunty who prayed to my father, also come to know about my rocky heart state. So one fine day she invited and forced me to attend the Meeting at the church once. It was day of Christmas, Dec 25-2012. I visited the church, sat inside prayer hall near window beside door. The messenger God servant preaching the Biblical verses regarding the confession, repentance and sacrifice of Jesus Christ to save us from the deadly sin which we cannot blot ourselves. How lord Jesus Christ offered himself on cross, depicted clearly the painful situation underwent by Lord Jesus just to save us. When he was preaching with a full of spirit, I felt he is directly speaking to me. Then I don't know what happened the tears rolled out and my rocky heart started melting, slowly converting into fleshy heart. The preacher said these word to accept and invite Lord Jesus Christ into your heart as below, a simple A-B–C formula

A- **Accept** *Lord Jesus Christ as your personal savior*

B- **Believe** *Lord Jesus Christ died for you.*

C- **Confess** *you are sinner*

The same thing I prayed in my heart, and accepted, invited Lord Jesus Christ as my personal savior. That day I was reborn in Christ and became child of God.Then I also started believing my Lord Jesus Christ for the miracle done by God before my sight and made me as a witness of his great works in our life. Lord took us into this kind of tough situation and opened our eyes of our mind and made us to realize the true God.

I gave my testimony in the waters of Baptism on 25th Feb, 2015 before all the people of God declaring myself as Child of Living God. I started to read daily bible portion out of my KJV bible. I continued to be a regular visitor of Church in my home town attending the Sunday Worships, Youth Meetings, Special meetings. I started to spend some of my time in service to God on sundays, Any meetings in Church, in which I felt more happiness.

I noticed much changes in my life, as the days are passing. I found the differences when I compared to my present and past life practically before my eyes when i think of it. When I pass before any temples my sight or thoughts or any part of my mind never tried to look at it. These are all the signs indicates that you are saved and reborn, became a born-again Child of God.

Final Conclusion

15

Lord used my father as a tool to bring salvation to my home, honored my mother's faith and did miracle before me, took us into a way of salvation and transformed our lives, blotting out our iniquities, adorned with a garments of salvation. Finally we became Gods child.

This is how Lord Jesus Christ observed the Mustard seed of faith in my mother and heard her prayer and performed his acts before our eyes and took hold of us (my family) and helped in all the situation that we come across from that time onwards my whole family believed in Christ and followed him. Lord Jesus Christ granted salvation to my family through the faith of my mother in Christ.

THUS WE ACCEPTED JESUS CHRIST AS SAVIOR, OUR LIVING GOD.

MY FAMILY ALWAYS THANKFUL TO LORD FOR SAVING US.

Gods Plan Strategy To Bring My Family Under Salvation